AF587488

PEGASUS ENCYCLOPEDIA

MARINE MAMMALS

Edited by: Pallabi B. Tomar, Hitesh Iplani
Managing editor: Tapasi De
Designed by: Vijesh Chahal, Anil Kumar, Rohit Kumar
Illustrated by: Suman S. Roy, Tanoy Choudhury
Colouring done by: Vinay Kumar, Sonu, Kiran Kumari & Pradeep Kumar

CONTENTS

What are mammals?

Mammals are warm-blooded vertebrates that evolved in the Jurassic Period, about 175 million years ago. They evolved from reptiles. Common mammals include rodents, bats, dogs, bears, cats, deer, sheep, goats and humans. In all, there are about 5,400 species of mammals.

Animals with vertebrate are those animals which have a spine (backbone). Not all animals have a backbone. Being warm-blooded means the bodies of mammals are built to maintain just about the same temperature all the time irrespective of their cold or hot environments. This feature has enabled mammals to survive in all sorts of places from the tropics to the poles.

What are marine mammals?

Most mammals are terrestrial. However, there are some mammals that either fully live in the oceans or mostly live in the oceans. Whales and dolphins live completely in the sea. The otter, the walrus, seal live mostly in the sea, feeding in the oceans and breeding on the shores. These mammals that live in the sea are known as **marine mammals**.

Marine mammals have the same characteristics as all other mammals, the only difference being that they have adapted to living all or part of their life in the oceans.

The most well-known marine mammals are the dolphins and the blue whales. Other than these species, marine mammals include seals, sea otters, walrus and polar bears. Statistically speaking, there are 120 species of mammals which either inhabit the oceans or depend on the ocean floor for food.

Even though they live in the sea, marine mammals do not get their oxygen from the water around them. Like fishes they don't have gills which can process oxygen from water. Instead, they come to the surface after some amount of time in order to breathe. Then they hold their breath and dive underwater.

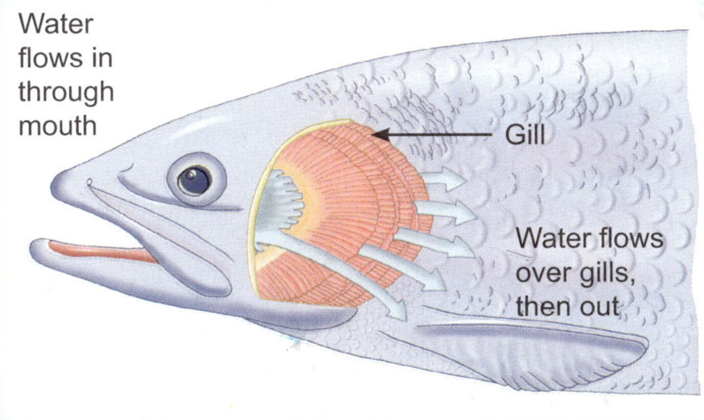

The time period of the dive differs for every species. Marine mammals have almost all the characteristics of mammals differing only in the habitat.

Marine mammals have been divided into five groups:

- **Cetaceans** (whales, dolphins, and porpoises),
- **Pinnipeds** (seals, sea lions, fur seals, and walruses)
- **Sirenians** (dugongs and manatees)
- **Sea otters**
- **Polar bears**

The largest group of marine mammals are the whales and dolphins with about 86 species. Polar bears are not marine mammals in the strictest sense of the term. However, they display certain characteristics which are peculiar to marine mammals and also because of the key role they play in the marine ecosystem in the polar areas, they are considered as marine mammals.

Unfortunately, many marine mammals are considered endangered species and there are many threats to most of their populations such as illegal hunting, pollution, climate change and habitat loss.

Origin and evolution

For evolutionists, the origin of marine mammals has been one of the most difficult issues to explain. There are many contradicting theories that have been proposed by scientists to understand the evolution of marine mammals.

According to one theory, about 65 million years ago when dinosaurs became extinct and opportunities for food opened up on land, some animals, including the dolphins and whales, moved onshore to take advantage of the food supply.

For some reason, probably again to find food, the descendants of these animals worked their way back into the sea, probably first dwelling on shore before becoming full-fledged ocean dwellers.

So, according to this theory, marine mammals evolved from their land dwelling ancestors over time by developing adaptations to life in the water.

The fossil record for whales is not as extensive as it is for other marine mammals such as otters and pinnipeds. So, the transition period between land and water is unclear.

Due to the lack of complete and clear evidence and the theory's unclear, contradictory and confusing nature, evolutionists have been silent on this issue for a long time. However, the research on the issue is still going on.

The remains of **Ambulocetus natans**, whose name means 'walking whale that swam', dating 49 million years ago were found in Pakistan in 1994. According to these remains, the animal once had strong legs with long feet, similar to modern pinnipeds, which were functional both on land and in the sea.

Types of marine mammals

Cetaceans

The word cetacean is used to describe all whales, dolphins and porpoises in the order **Cetacea**. This word comes from the Latin word cetus which means 'large sea animal' and the Greek word ketos which means 'sea monster'.

There are about 86 species of cetaceans and more species are still being discovered.

Cetaceans surface after regular intervals to exhale carbon dioxide and inhale a fresh supply of oxygen. A blowhole is present on the top of their bodies which remains closed during diving. When the cetacean surfaces again for oxygen, the muscles open the blowholes and warm air is exhaled.

Humpback whale

Whales

Whales are the largest animals that have ever lived on Earth and are the largest animals that live in the ocean. Whales are even bigger than the largest dinosaur. The biggest whale is the blue whale, which grows to be about 30 m long. These enormous animals eat about 4 tons of tiny krill each day!

Blue whale

Bottlenose Dolphin

Dolphins

Dolphins are found in both rivers and seas. All dolphins are toothed whales belonging to the sub-order, **odontocetes**, of the order cetacean. There are almost 40 species of dolphin. They vary in size from 1.2 m and 40 kg (Maui's Dolphin) upto 9.5 m and 10 tons (the Orca).

Porpoises

Porpoises are cetaceans belonging to the family Phocoenidae. They are the smallest of the toothed whales. There are six species of porpoise. They inhabit all oceans except the Arctic and Antarctic. Porpoises resemble the dolphin, but are smaller—seldom more than 1.8 m long—and have a blunt muzzle instead of a pointed one.

Pinnipeds

The word 'pinniped' is a Latin word which means 'fin-footed'. Pinnipeds are found all over the world. The pinnipeds include all the seals and the walruses.

There are three families of pinnipeds—the **Phocidae**, the earless or 'true' seals, the **Otariidae**, the eared seals (sea lion and fur seals), and the **Odobenidae**, the walrus. These three families contain 33 species.

Odobenidae

The walrus is the only living species in the **Odobenidae** family. There are three subspecies of the species walrus: the **Atlantic Walrus**, the **Pacific Walrus** and **O. rosmarus laptevi**, which lives in the Laptev Sea. Like phocidae, it lacks external ears. The walrus is recognized by its huge tusks, whiskers and great bulk.

Otariidae

Eared seals or Otariidae comprise 16 species in seven genera. Eared seals have small external earflaps and hind flippers that can be turned to face forwards. They are commonly known either as sea lions or fur seals. Sea lions are larger and have coarse, short fur in contrast to a dense underfur of fur seal.

Phocidae

Most **earless seals** are found in the cold waters of the Arctic and Antarctic. Some live under ice most of the time, finding cracks and holes in the ice through which to breath. True seals have ear holes but no external ear flaps.

Sirenians

Sirenians are animals which include manatees and dugongs. The Steller's sea cow, which is now extinct, is also a part of this group.

Dugong

The sirenians are primarily found along the coasts and inland waterways of the United States, Central and South America, West Africa, Asia and Australia.

Manatees

Manatees are the only marine mammals that are herbivores. Although they may resemble whales and dolphins, they are actually more closely related to elephants. There are 3 species of manatees.

In ancient mythology, 'siren' was a term used for monsters or sea nymphs who lured sailors and their ships with mesmerizing songs. Throughout history, sailors sometimes thought they were seeing mermaids when they were probably seeing manatees or dugongs.

Dugong

Dugongs are also known as 'sea cows' because they graze on sea grass and the roots of aquatic plants. There is only one dugong species living today, which is simply called the dugong. The name 'Dugong' comes from the Malay word 'duyong', which means 'lady of the sea' or 'mermaid'.

Mustelids

The mustelids are the group of mammals that include weasels, otters and badgers. Not all of them are marine mammals. Of these only two species in this group are found in marine habitats—the sea otter, which lives in the Pacific coastal areas from Alaska to California and in Russia; and the sea cat or the marine otter which lives along the Pacific coast of South America.

Otter

Sea otters are the smallest marine mammal but the largest and heaviest of all the otters. Unlike other marine mammals, they don't have a thick layer of blubber under their skin. Instead, they have thick fur with upto 1 million hairs per square inch of their body.

Polar Bear

The polar bear is the only bear considered to be a marine mammal primarily because it lives on sea ice for most or all of the year. Also, they are great swimmers and their forepaws are partially webbed. They also have a thick layer of blubber and excellent underwater vision. Their nostrils close while diving.

The polar bear lives only in the Northern Hemisphere, on the arctic ice cap, and spends most of its time in coastal areas.

Differences between marine mammals and other sea animals

There are many differences between sea mammals and other sea life which have been discussed below:

1. Mammals swim by moving their spine up and down, while sea fish swim by moving their spine sideways.
2. Marine mammals come to the surface to breathe air, whereas other sea animals take oxygen from water.
3. Unlike other marine animals, marine mammals maintain a high internal body temperature. The thick blubber, fur and the air bubbles between skin and water helps them to maintain the high body temperature.
4. Marine mammals give birth to their ofsprings and the female produces milk to feed them. They give birth to one calf or pup at a time. The milk from female marine mammals generally exceeds 40-50 per cent fat content which helps the young to develop the blubber.
5. Unlike other sea animals, marine mammals have hair on their body. The cetaceans have little bristles around the head or mouth. The thickness of the hair coat varies. Some cetaceans don't have hair. The thickness of hair is more in polar bears and sea otters than in sea lions.

Unique characteristics and adaptations

Water conservation

Marine mammals are unable to meet their water requirements in the same way as fish do, by using salt water. They need freshwater in order to survive.

Although, the water source of marine animals is not well-known, it is believed that they meet a large part of their water requirements through their food.

They also possess water conservation mechanisms like that seen in camels. Like camels, marine mammals do not sweat. They have specialized kidneys that produces urine that is saltier than the seawater.

Whales can stay underwater without breathing for an hour or more! It is possible because they make very efficient use of their lungs, exchanging up to 90 per cent air of their lung volume with each breath. They also store unusually high amounts of oxygen in their blood and muscles when diving.

Oxygen

Fish and other organisms that live underwater get their oxygen from water, either through their gills or their skin. Marine mammals, on the other hand, need to come to the water surface to breathe, which is why the deep-diving whales have blowholes on top of their heads, so they can surface to breathe while keeping most of their body underwater.

Body temperature

Many sea animals are cold-blooded (**ectothermic**) and their internal body temperature is the same as their surrounding environment. Marine mammals, however, are warm-blooded (**endothermic**), which means they need to keep their internal body temperature constant.

To achieve that marine mammals have an insulating layer of blubber (made up of fat and connective tissue) under their skin. This layer allows them to keep their internal body temperature about the same as ours even in the cold ocean. This layer is thinner in warmer temperatures and thicker in colder climates.

Another technique to regulate body temperature is hauling. Seals and other marine mammals often haul themselves on the beach to take a sun bath to warm their bodies.

Sight

In a marine environment, sea mammals are faced with factors like salt level, increasing pressure while deep diving and marine currents. All these factors can cause problems in their sight.

To combat these factors the eyes of marine mammals are positioned on the sides of the head in order to avoid direct contact with the current.

The Bowhead Whale living in the Arctic waters, has a blubber layer that is 2 feet thick!

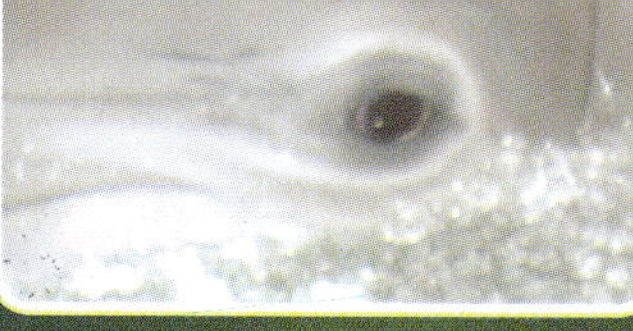

In addition, marine mammals have a hard membrane to protect the eye during deep dives. Other adaptations that these mammals show are spherical eye lens, more light-sensitive rod cells instead of cone cells, which are sensitive to colour and detail.

Communication

Unlike land mammals, hearing is much more important to the marine mammals. Since underwater visibility and light levels can change and many whales and dolphins hunt in the dark depths of the sea, whales and some other marine mammals do not rely on sight to find their food. Instead, they locate prey using echolocation and their hearing.

What is echolocation?

To put it simply, echolocation is the method of determining the location of an object by measuring the time taken by an echo to travel back to its source after hitting that object.

Sound waves are focused and sent to one point. The returning waves are then analyzed and interpreted in the animal's brain. This analysis quite clearly gives an idea about the shape, size, speed and position of an object.

This technique helps them to see in murky waters, avoiding obstacle and finding prey and fellow companions. Their echolocation system or 'sonar system' is very sensitive.

Toothed whales in particular are able to 'see' by means of the sound waves returning to them. Dolphins use sound waves for communication as well as for direction-finding. Two whales, even hundreds of kilometres apart, can communicate by the use of sound. On land, bats use similar technique.

A dolphin's skull is especially sound-proofed to protect its brain from being damaged by the sound waves it emits constantly and powerfully.

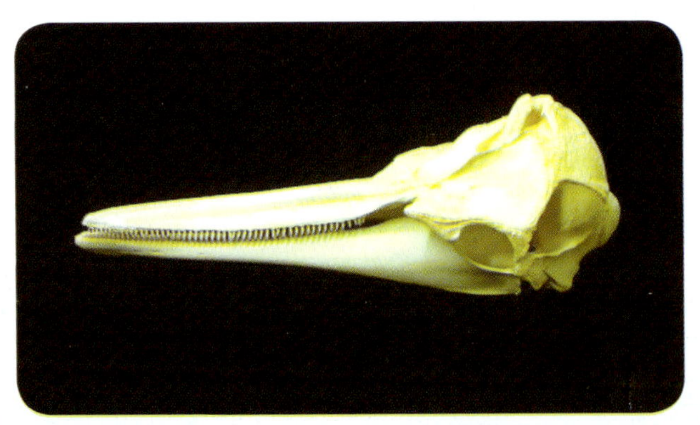

Streamlined body

Marine mammals have a streamlined shape for efficient movement through water. The lack of fur coat on several marine mammals is an important advantage to swimming as smooth skin causes less friction than fur.

Other than that, absence of protruding ears, dorsal fin for balance, side flippers for balance and steering, tail fluke's up and down movement provides powerful propulsion through the water.

Sperm Whales can dive for more than 1,600 m and may remain underwater for an hour or more! The Elephant Seal can dive for more than 1,500 m and can stay underwater for two hours.

Deep diving

Since marine mammals have to come to the surface to breathe they have a lot of features which help them in diving at great depths for longer period of time.

- Apart from their lungs being able to retain more oxygen, their blood chemistry as well allows them to retain greater amount of oxygen in their blood. Also, the proteins in their muscles use and store oxygen efficiently.
- Marine mammals have a high tolerance to carbon dioxide. Their muscles can work without oxygen for a long time while they hold their breath.
- While diving, blood flow is restricted from the parts that can handle low oxygen levels such as muscles of the fins; and instead is directed towards the heart and brain where oxygen is needed the most.

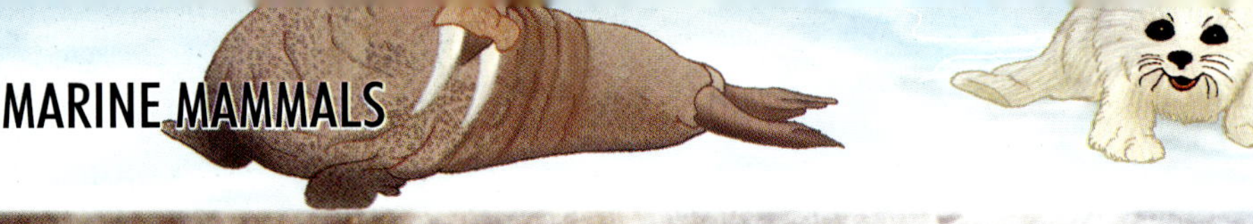

Counter-shading

- Their bodies are well adapted to tolerate tremendous atmospheric pressure at great depths.
- During a dive, their bodies reduce the rate of the heartbeat so that less oxygen is needed to pump blood to the body parts.

Camouflage

Another important characteristic displayed by most marine mammals is **counter-shading**. It is a sort of colouring of the body in which the upper part of the body, which is visible from above, while swimming is dark coloured and the lower part of the body, which is visible from below, is light in colour.

This sort of colouring hides the animal from being viewed by predators. During swimming, the dark top of the body blends in with the dark colour of the sea. When seen from below, the light-coloured belly blends in with the sunlit surface.

Habitat and food

Marine mammals are found in the oceans. The oceans cover more than two-thirds of the globe, providing a home to at least, 118 species of marine mammals.

The marine biome comprises of the Antarctic Ocean, the Arctic Ocean, the Indian Ocean, the Atlantic Ocean and the Pacific Ocean, plus smaller Bays and Gulfs. Also, it consists of 80 per cent of all the Earth's habitats, making it the largest habitat on our planet.

The marine biome can also be divided into oceans, estuaries and coral reefs with the oceans representing the most diverse and largest of ecosystems.

Baleens, which are large stiff plates that grow down from the gums of the whale's upper jaw, allow whales to filter their food.

Baleen is made of **keratin**, the same protein that makes up hair and fingernails and is strong, yet flexible. The whale filters plankton, krill and small fish from seawater by squeezing water through the baleen with its tongue and then licking the plankton off the baleen.

Baleens

Cetaceans are near the top of the marine food chain and are classified into two groups— those with **teeth** and those with **baleens**.

Astonishing fact

Beaked Whales have an extraordinary ability to dive into great depths (they are seldom seen at the surface); 1,899 metres and possibly more, making them the deepest diving air-breathing animals known!

Manatee

Toothed whales are hunters and use their teeth to grasp their prey, but do not chew their food. They eat fish, squid and other marine mammals. Manatees and dugongs are herbivores. They only eat vegetation, such as sea grasses, algae, mangrove leaves and water hyacinths.

Pinnipeds (seals, sea lions and walrus) have teeth that are sharp and good for grabbing fish and other food such as shellfish. Like the toothed whales, pinnipeds do not chew their food, but swallow it whole or in big chunks.

Sea otters typically float on their backs while eating, using their chest as a dining table. A tool such as a stone is used to break open the hard shells of their prey (clams and crabs) or to knock shellfish off rocks. This is one of the few known cases of animal using tools.

The sea otters have flat molars for grinding and eating mostly benthic (bottom-dwelling) invertebrates (animals with no backbones), such as clams, mussels, urchins, crabs and abalone.

Sea Otter

A polar bear's favourite food is seal. If there are no seals to hunt, they will eat small whales, lemmings and even geese.

Some well-known marine mammals

Blue Whale

The blue whale is the largest animal that has ever lived on Earth. The largest recorded length of a blue whale is 33 m, but sizes generally range from 24-30 m. An average weight for an adult is 100-150 tons. Its heart alone is as large as a small car! Blue whales are an overall blue-gray colour, mottled with light gray.

Blue whales are found in every ocean of the world. Blue whales swim individually or in small groups. The favourite food of these giants is krill or shrimp-like euphausiids that are up to three inches long.

Blue whales are the loudest animals on Earth. They are even louder than a jet engine. Their low frequency whistle can be heard for hundreds of miles, and is probably used to attract other blue whales.

Killer Whale (Orca)

The orca or killer whale is a toothed whale and is the largest member of the dolphin family. Orcas grow to be about 8-10 m long, weighing more than 6 tons. Orcas have long, rounded bodies with large dorsal fins on the middle of their backs. Their black bodies are marked with white patches on the underside and near the eyes.

Killer whales eat fish, squid, sea turtles, sea birds and other marine mammals including seals and dolphins. Packs of killer whales are capable of killing and eating a blue whale.

The killer whale is found in all the oceans of the world. It usually stays in areas with colder temperature.

Maui's Dolphin

Maui's dolphin is the world's smallest dolphin and is found only on the west coast of the North Island of New Zealand and nowhere else in the world. With less than 150 left in the wild, it is New Zealand's rarest dolphin. Females produce one calf every 2-4 years, making population increase very slow. They are about 1.7 m long and weigh up to 50 kg.

The dolphin is listed internationally as 'critically endangered', which means there is a high risk of it becoming extinct in the near future.

Amazon River Dolphin

There are five species of dolphins that make their homes in rivers, but the most popular of them are the pink Amazon River dolphins, also known as Boto or Boutu.

Among the five species of river dolphins, Amazon pink dolphins are considered the most intelligent, with a brain capacity 40 per cent larger than that of humans.

Pink dolphins inhabit the Amazon River, but they can also be found in the Orinoco basin and the upper Madeira River as well. While they are mostly pink, these dolphins have various coloured skins, which can be light gray, pink or brown. It is between 2.5 to 3 m long and weigh about 90 kg. Males are generally larger.

Narwhal

The 'unicorn of the ocean,' the narwhal is one of the rarest whales in the world. Narwhals are very elusive and mysterious in nature, and are very distinct in appearance due to the large horn-like tusk on its face. The tusk is actually a tooth that grows from the upper jaw of male narwhals. They range in size from 4 to 6.1 m and weigh upto 1600 kg.

Narwhals live in the icy waters of the Arctic seas. They rarely stray far from ice. Most narwhals travel in pods of 10-100 individuals and sometimes in much larger groups. They communicate with various sounds like squeals, trills and clicks. The males often cross tusks in a behaviour known as 'tusking'.

Steller's Sea Cow

The Steller's sea cow was a large sirenian mammal. It was discovered in 1741 near the Asiatic coast of the Bering Sea by German biologist Georg Steller, who was travelling with the explorer Vitus Bering. Just 28 years later, the species was extinct. It is the first recorded example of humans driving a marine species to extinction.

Steller's sea cows were the largest and the only cold-water members of the scientific order Sirenia, to which manatees and dugongs also belong. Feeding on sea grasses, they were the only aquatic herbivorous mammals. As the largest sirenian, it reached a length of 9–10 m and a weight of perhaps 10 metric tons much larger than present-day manatees and dugongs.

Leopard Seal

The leopard seal is the second largest species of seal in the world (behind the elephant seal). They have a body length between 2.5 and 3.2 m and weigh between 200 and 455 kg. The bull leopard seal (male leopard seal) is generally smaller than the female leopard seal with large males growing to around 3m.

The leopard seal is a dominant predator in its environment and is rarely preyed upon by other animals with the exception of human hunters. They are found in the Antarctic and sub-Antarctic waters. They mainly feed upon smaller seals, penguins, other birds, fish, squid and krill.

Giant Otter

The giant otter is the longest of all the otter species, with a length of 1.8m, including the tail and a weight of 34 kg. The females are smaller and weigh only 26-27 kg. The fur is dense, thick and velvety and is highly sought after by fur traders. The fur is water repellent and is a deep chocolate brown in colour. A unique white mark is located on the throat that can be used to distinguish between individuals. The head is round and the ears are small. The nose is completely covered in fur, with only the two slit-like nostrils visible. The eyes are large and acute, perfect for hunting underwater. The giant otter is well suited for an aquatic life, and can close its ears while underwater.

Giant otters are only found in the rainforests and rivers of South America. They tend to set up their nests on the banks of slow moving rivers and lakes as this is safer for their young.

Ross Seal

The Ross seal is a small, rarely seen seal that breeds and rests on Antarctica pack ice. They have a loud call that is often likened to a siren. Ross seals have a body length between 1.7 and 3 m and they weigh between 130 and 215 kg. They have a slender body and a thick neck. They are dark grey/brown in colour and have very large eyes.

Ross seals primarily eat squid, other cephalopods, fish and krill. They typically forage at depths of 100 to 200 m, but may go deeper, especially at twilight. Predators of Ross seals include killer whales and leopard seals.

Dall's Porpoise

Often called the 'spray' porpoise, Dall's porpoises are the fastest of all the porpoises. This porpoise swims at such high speeds – up to 55 km/h that observers often see only the cone-shaped water spray kicked up by its head, rather than the porpoise itself.

Dall's were named after an American naturalist, W. H. Dall, who was the first person to identify the species. They are 1.7-2.2 m long and are extremely stocky and powerful. They have a varied diet and feed on squid, jack mackerel, hake, capelin crustaceans and herring. It mostly feeds at night.

Dall's are generally found in the North Pacific and South Bering Sea. Groups of 2-20 have been seen, although there have been sightings of groups of several thousand. The only natural enemies of Dall's, other than man, are killer whales and occasionally sharks.

Test Your MEMORY

1. What are marine mammals?
2. Write briefly about the origin and evolution of marine mammals.
3. Write the types of marine mammals.
4. Name the two sirenians.
5. Write two differences between marine mammals and other sea animals.
6. Describe some unique characteristics of marine mammals.
7. What is echolocation?
8. What is counter-shading?
9. Name the largest animal that has ever lived on Earth.
10. Describe Narwhals.
11. Write a few lines about the Steller's sea cow.
12. Name the second largest species of seal in the world.

Index